I0760000

LANDSCAPE
OBSERVER
LONDON
VLADIMIR GUCULAK
jovis

Foreword

Landscape Observer: London is focused on promoting and documenting excellence in external public spaces across London. The UK capital has been undergoing a substantial urban transformation in the past fifteen years with a big focus on improving the public realm across its thirty-two boroughs. Extensive infrastructure and housing market investments are fuelling the need for a range of quality public spaces. Changes include the creation of new public spaces and good quality housing, revitalization of brownfields, strengthening of communities, and upgrading of existing parklands and gardens.

Like many other cities across Europe, London's landscape is transforming. It's former industrial sites are becoming prime spots for future developemnts. The need for quality residential accomodation and a growing demand for office and retail space is challenging developers to build in the most complex urban conditions. Vast post–industrial landscapes around Battersea power station, King's Cross Station, Paddington Basin, and Stratford are becoming popular spots for new developments. The success or failure of the new urban developments is very much dependent on the quality of open public space.

Landscape Observer: London provides an overview of eighty-nine projects that were implemented in the last years, ranging in scale, programme, and budget. Photographs capture the spaces in their everyday set up and operation and details of the hard and soft landscape elements are labelled to provide readers with essential information on key materials and plants used in each individual project.

This book is an attempt to represent a first account of the new landscape projects in London. It may fail to recognise all of the most recent projects or correctly identify all the planting or materials used in various schemes, but hopefully it will fullfill its main purpose, to encourage people to go outside, observe and study surrounding environments, travel to London, explore and experience wonderful places.

This is an atlas of contemporary landscape architecture in London, a reference guide and source of inspiration for landscape architects, urban planners, garden designers, and political activists in the field of infrastructure and urban planning. It provides suggestions for city walks through the various districts of London.

Foreword

While providing no direct judgement or analysis of the showcased public spaces there are some obvious trends and conclusions that became apparent in the process of putting this book together.

- Sucessful public oben spaces are not always designed by landscape architects. Garden designers, architects, and horticulture experts play very important roles in shaping the public realm.

- Delivering a good public project is dependant on succeeding at three stages: design, construction, and maintenance. A succesful result cannot be achieved if one the stages fails.

- Most of recent public spaces in London represent exampels of private-public partnerships, where private developers are offering to provide public access to privately managed sites.

- The details and materials of hard landscape elements of the public landscape projects in London seem to follow a certain pallette that challenges designers and puts added pressure on delivering exemplary planting schemes that often have a huge impact on your experience of the landscape.

- Scale of a project does not impact its success.

Readers are welcomed to make their own judgements and encouraged to observe and record the changes to their surroundings. Learning from the good examples and memorable experiences together with the ability to distinguish failures will help us to shape a better environment.

Table of Contents

London – Map

14
9
6
3
10
8
12
59
64
58
63
16
20
13
60
54
21
55
57
17
22
61
56
23
62
69
68
65
66
67

44
49
46
5
43
47
38
45
2
1
52
42
11
36
35
28
37
34
32
29
33
27
24
26
18
30
31
25
78
84
53
48
82
50
36
77
41
40
72
83
81
74
79
51
86
75
39
71
87
73
89
88

North

1

1. London – North

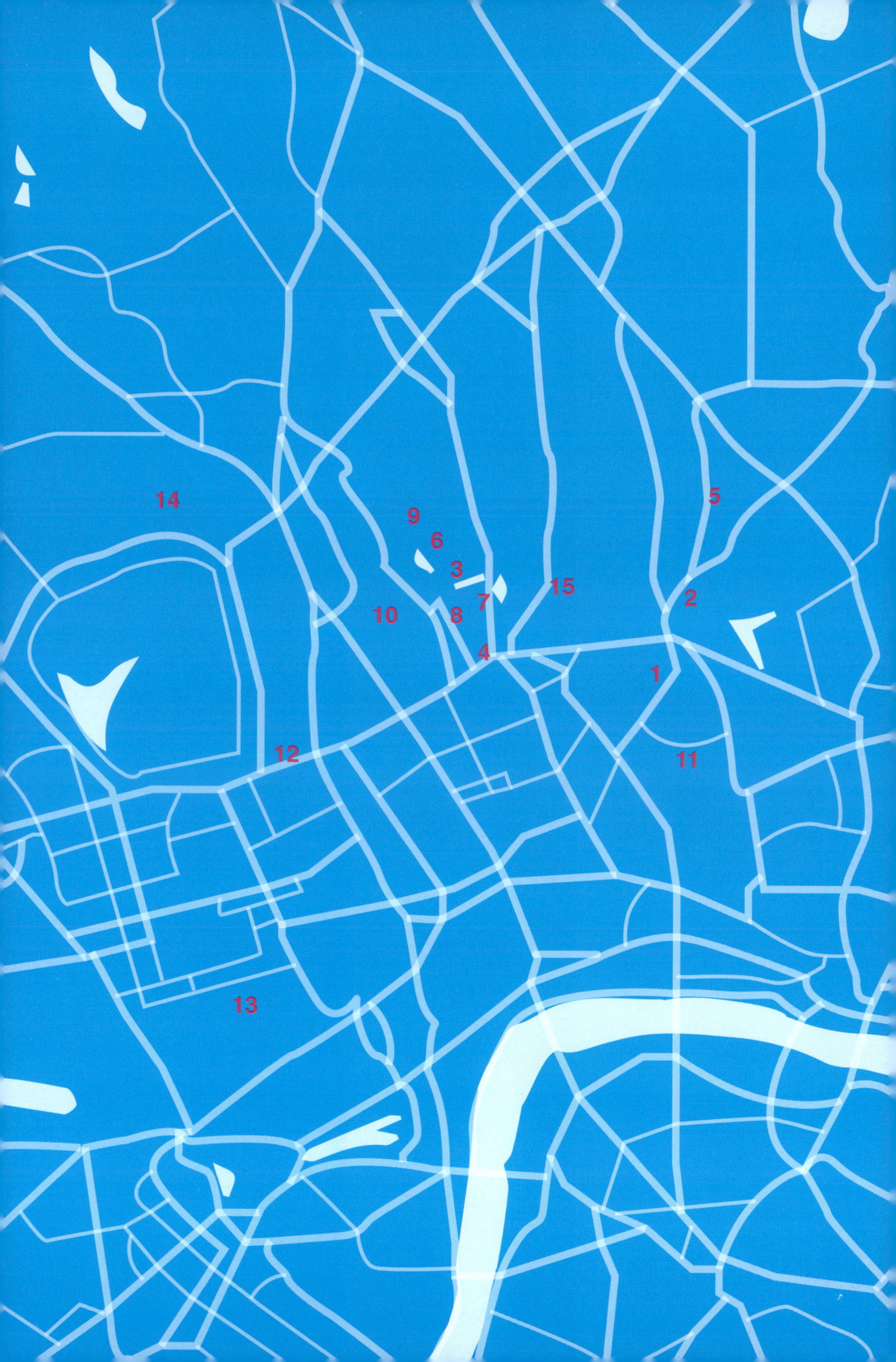

14
9
6
3
15
5
2
7
10
8
4
1
11
12
13

Angel Building

Portuguese granite setts with a line of mature *Plantanus x acerifolia*

Angel Building

Location:	Islington
Site Area:	> 500 m^2
Completion:	2010
Designer:	J&L Gibbons
Transport:	Angel tube
Open:	24/7

1 - Portuguese granite bench
2 - Granite edge and box hedge
3 - Stainless steel cycle hoops
4 - Portuguese granite setts and flags
5 - Tree pit detail
6 - Building uplighter
7 - Signage
8 - Portuguese granite bench
9 - Portable street furniture

Duncan Terrace Gardens

1 - Precast, pigmented concrete retaining edge unit embossed with a rose motif
2 - *Phlox paniculata*
3 - *Persicaria amplexicaulis*
4 - Timber benches detail
5 - Timber benches
6 - Timber poles, wire fence
7 - Raised lawn area
8 - Art installation by artists Bruce Gilchrist and Jo Joelson of "London Fieldworks"
9 - Precast concrete retaining edge

Duncan Terrace Gardens

Location:	Islington
Site Area:	> 3,000 m^2
Completion:	2010
Designer:	remapp Landscape Architects
Transport:	Angel Station
Open:	24/7

1 - Oak bench detail
2 - Bench armrest
3 - Solid oak bench
4 - Brick and balustrade interface
5 - Balustrade detail
6 - Corner of the balustrade
7 - Corner detail
8 - Handrail setting out
9 - Gate fixing detail

Granary Square & Regent's Canal

Location:	Islington
Site Area:	> 1,000 m^2
Completion:	2010
Designer:	Dan Pearson Studio, Townshend Landscape
Transport:	Angel tube
Open:	24/7

Granary Square & Regent's Canal

Granary Square & Regent's Canal

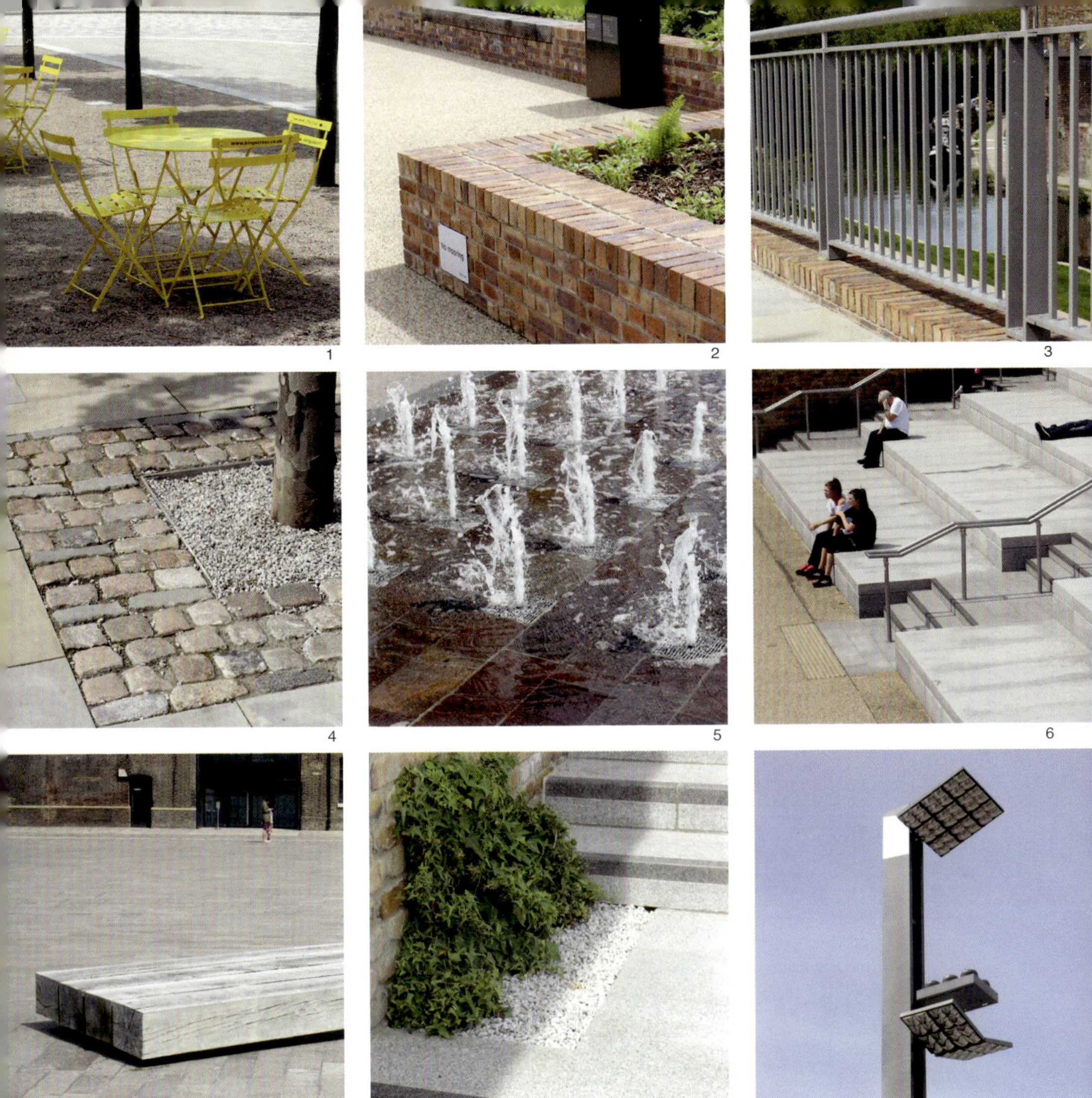

7 8 9

1 - Flexible furniture, Cedec
2 - Brick planter
3 - Steel balustrade
4 - Reclaimed granite setts, Yorkstone slabs, steel edge and gravel tree pit
5 - Jets fountain, porphyry paving
6 - Granite terrace with steps
7 - Solid oak bench
8 - Ivy
9 - LED light post

Granary Square & Regent's Canal

Granary Square & Regent's Canal

1 - Water feature drainage channel, porphyry paving
2 - Mixed granite paving
3 - Granite kerb edge
4 - Reclaimed granite setts and industrial relics
5 - Feature stone paving with embedded lettering
6 - Drainage gully
7 - Granite seat
8 - Reused granite setts and old railway tracks
9 - Grey granite steps with black granite inserts

Granary Square & Regent's Canal

Granary Square & Regent's Canal

Granary Square & Regent's Canal

Granary Square & Regent's Canal

Granary Square & Regent's Canal

Brunnera macrophylla, ferns, Amelanchier lamarckii

1

2

3

4

King's Cross Square

Location:	King's Cross
Site Area:	7,000 m^2
Completion:	2013
Designer:	Stanton Williams
Transport:	King's Cross St. Pancras Station
Open:	24/7

1 - *Sophora japonica* in raised granite planters
2 - Tree grill with integrated uplighters
3 - Wayfinding totems
4 - Lighting column

King's Cross Square

The welfare of the growing trees has been assured by deploying the GreenBlue Urban StrataCell structural modular soil management system.

Handyside Gardens

1

2

3

4

5

Handyside Gardens

Location:	King's Cross
Site Area:	> 1,000 m^2
Completion:	2015
Designer:	Dan Pearson Studio
Transport:	King's Cross St. Pancras station
Open:	24/7

1 - Corten planter edge, water feature, *Fragaria vesca, Melica altissima*

2 - *Acer campestre, Epimedium*

3 - Raised planter, *Erigeron karvinskianus, Ajuga reptans, Bergenia cordifolia*

4 - *Ajuga reptans, Bergenia cordifolia*

5 - Timber bench detail

1 - *Stachys byzantina*

2 - Hardwood timber bench detail

3 - Corten planter edge, box hedge, water feature

4 - *Tellima grandiflora*

5 - Corten planter edge

6 - *Erigeron karvinskianus, Lavandula angustifolia*

7 - *Tellima grandiflora*

8 - *Erigeron karvinskianus, Lavandula angustifolia*

9 - Bespoke timber lounge chairs

Handyside Gardens

1

2

3

4

Lewis Cubitt Park

Location:	King's Cross
Site Area:	> 500 m^2
Completion:	2016
Designer:	Townshend Landscape Architects
Transport:	King's Cross St. Pancras Station
Open:	24/7

1 - Granite paved square with a series of water feature and seating areas

2 - Water jet

3 - Bespoke timber bench

4 - Rusty concrete planters

Lewis Cubitt Park

Plantanus x acerifolia, multistem Aescalus, Erigeron karvinskianus, Lavandula angustifolia, Epimedium, Heleborus

1 - *Lavandula angustifolia*
2 - *Miscanthus*
3 - *Miscanthus, Erigeron karvinskianus, Arbutus unedo*
4 - Handmade clay pots
5 - *Erigeron karvinskianus*
6 - *Salvia microphylia*
7 - *Phillyrea angustifolia*
8 - Clipped *Phillyrea angustifolia*
9 - *Erigeron karvinskianus*

King's Cross Pots

Location:	King's Cross
Site Area:	> 500 m^2
Completion:	2016
Designer:	Dan Pearson Studio
Transport:	King's Cross St. Pancras Station
Open:	24/7

King's Cross Pots

1

2

3

4

Pancras Square

Location:	King's Cross
Site Area:	> 3,000 m^2
Completion:	2016
Designer:	Townshend Landscape Architects
Transport:	King's Cross St. Pancras Station
Open:	24/7

1 - A series of landscape terraces with lawns, planting beds and water feature
2 - Limestone clad water feature
3 - Flexible furniture
4 - *Liquidambar styraciflua*

Pancras Square

1 - Hardwood timber seat
2 - Brick paving
3 - Corten raised planter, *Salvia officinalis*
4 - *Luzula*
5 - Mint
6 - *Rubus*
7 - *Hedera* on steel cables
8 - *Betula*
8 - Hardwood timber seat

Gasholder Park

Location:	King's Cross
Site Area:	> 1,000 m^2
Completion:	2017
Designer:	Dan Pearson Studio
Transport:	King's Cross St. Pancras Station
Open:	24/7

Gasholder Park

1

2

3

4

1 - Corten raised planter with a hardwood timber seat

2 - *Salvia officinalis, Myrthus tarentina*

3 - *Libertia grandiflora*

4 - *Koelreuteria paniculata*

The Francis Circk Institute

1

2

3

4

5

The Francis Circk Institute

1 - Stainless steel planters
2 - Serpentine Yorkstone path with steel edges
3 - Stainless steel cables and supports for climbing plants
4 - Raised stainless steel edge
5 - Stainless steel planter with a timber bench

Location:	St. Pancras
Site Area:	< 500 m^2
Completion:	2016
Designer:	HOK, PLP Architecture
Transport:	King's Cross St. Pancras Station
Open:	24/7

1

2

3

4

Percival Triangle

Location:	Finsbury
Site Area:	< 500 m^2
Completion:	2009
Designer:	East
Transport:	Angel & Farringdon Stations
Open:	24/7

1 - Precast concrete planters
2 - Interlocking precast concrete edges
3 - Granite boulders
4 - Concrete kerb with gaps directs rainwater into the planted areas

Regent's Place

Regent's Place

Location:	Regent's Park
Site Area:	> 5,000 m^2
Completion:	2009
Designer:	EDCO Design
Transport:	Warren & Great Portland Street Stations
Open:	24/7

1 - Granite seating edge
2 - Steel lettering in granite paving
3 - Stylized ventilation grill
4 - Granite setts
5 - Stainless steel grill
6 - Tree pit with uplighters
7 - Steel pavilion by Carmody Groarke
8 - Granite setts and flush kerb
9 - Underplanted birch with uplighters

Regent's Place

Raised lawns and clipped yew hedge

Regent's Place

Westfield Green Wall

Location:	White City
Site Area:	> 1,000 m^2
Completion:	2016
Designer:	AECOM
Transport:	White City & Shepherd's Bush Stations
Open:	24/7

Westfield Green Wall

1

2

3

4

St Marks Church

Location:	Primrose Hill
Site Area:	> 500 m^2
Completion:	2016
Designer:	unknown
Transport:	Chalk Farm & Mornington Crescent Stations
Open:	24/7

1 - *Digitalis purpurea, Aquilegia vulgaris*
2 - *Convallaria majalis*
3 - *Aquilegia vulgaris*
4 - Irises

St Marks Church

St Marks Church

1

2

3

4

Vert Vertical Garden

Location:	King's Cross
Site Area:	< 500 m^2
Completion:	2013
Designer:	Neil Ayling, Clarke Associates
Transport:	King's Cross Station
Open:	24/7

1 - *Rosmarinus officinalis 'Prostratus'*
2 - Contrasting shard of painted metal
3 - Ferns and geraniums
4 - Folded shapes of origami-like steel planters

Central

2

2. London – Central

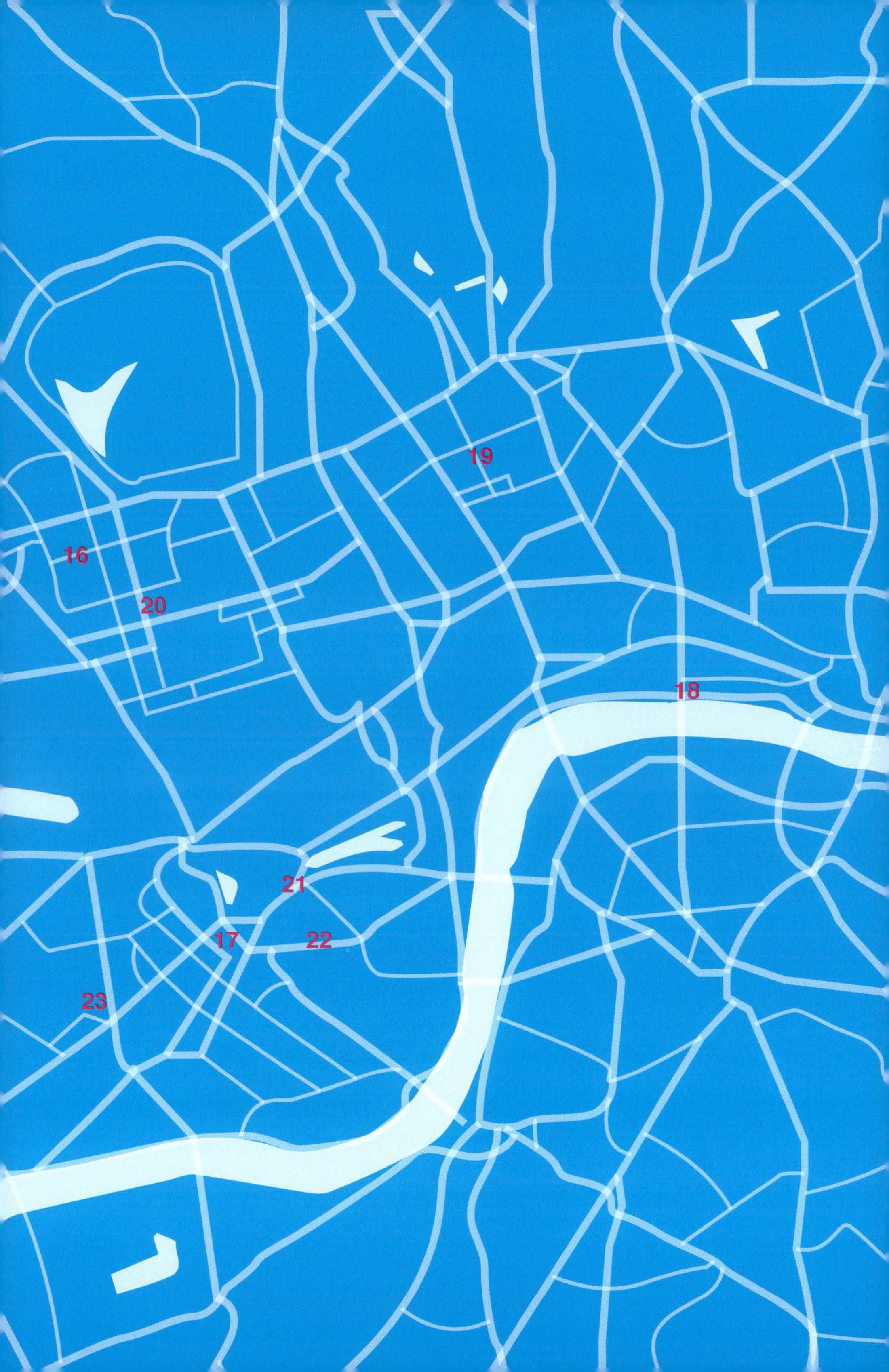
19
16
20
18
21
17
22
23

Brown Hart Gardens

CONSIDERATE
Improving the

Brown Hart Gardens

Brown Hart Gardens

Location:	Mayfair
Site Area:	< 1,000 m^2
Completion:	2013
Designer:	BDP
Transport:	Bond Street Station
Open:	24/7

1 - 1 mm Nordic Blue copper cassette panels
2 - Timber handrest
3 - Planter detail
4 - Glass and steel railing detail
5 - Railing interface with stone steps
6 - Water feature detail
7 - Steps and glass balustrade interface
8 - Limestone steps
9 - Handrail detail

Brown Hart Gardens

Phormium 'Apricot Queen', Skimmia japonica 'Rubella'

Brown Hart Gardens

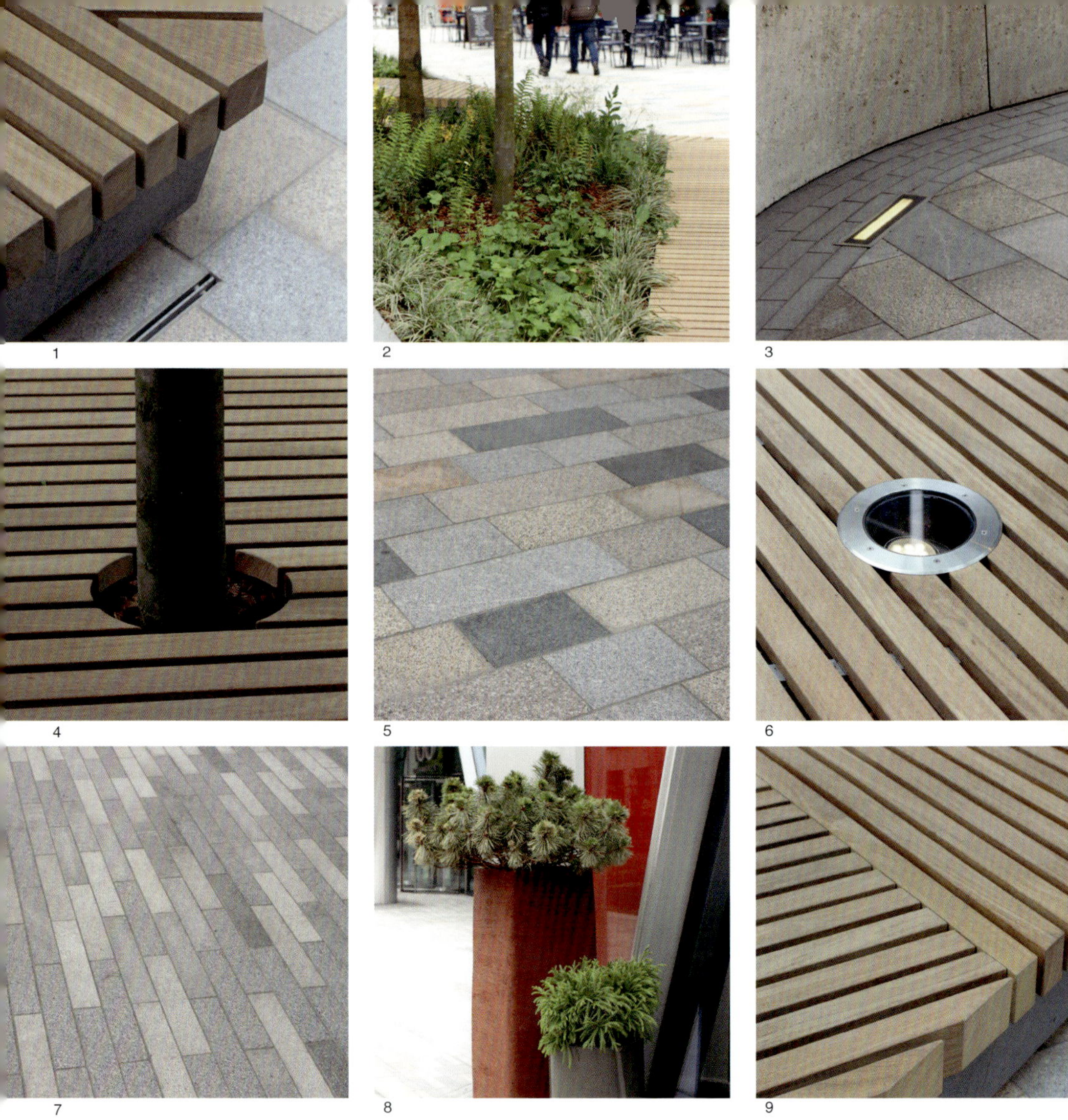

1 - Cumaru timber seat corner detail
2 - *Raised planter, Tellima grandiflora, Dryopteris affinis, Carex morrowii, Molinia caerulea*
3 - Combination of granite paving
4 - Tree pit detail within raised deck
5 - Granite paving, bush hammered finish
6 - Tree uplighter
7 - Mixed granite paving
8 - Pots
9 - Cumaru cladding for the seating areas

NOVA

Location:	Victoria
Site Area:	> 1,500 m^2
Completion:	2017
Designer:	PLP Architecture
Transport:	Victoria Station
Open:	24/7

NOVA

Tilia cordata in raised planters

1

2

3

4

Blackfriars Promenade

Location:	Temple
Site Area:	> 500 m^2
Completion:	2013
Designer:	Unknown
Transport:	Blackfriars Station
Open:	24/7

1 - Raised granite planter
2 - Terraced granite planters
3 - Granite seating edge
4 - Multistem birch

Marchmont Community Garden

1 - Steel fence
2 - Steel gate
3 - Composite timber decking, seating incorporated into retaining wall
4 - *Lavandula angustifolia* in a raised planter
5 - In-situ brushed concrete, composite timber decking
6 - Timber bench
7 - *Rosmarinus officinalis* in flower
8 - Timber seats and benches
9 - Mixed herbs

Marchmont Community Garden

Location:	Saint Pancras
Site Area:	< 500 m^2
Completion:	2011
Designer:	Architects Network
Transport:	Russel Square Station
Open:	24/7

Marchmont Community Garden

Origanum majorana, Lavandula angustifolia

Mount Street

1

2

3

4

Mount Street

Location:	Mayfair
Site Area:	< 500 m^2
Completion:	2011
Designer:	Tadao Ando, Blair Associates
Transport:	Bond Street & Marble Arch Stations
Open:	24/7

1 - Cloud of vapor around the base of existing London plane
2 - Polished granite edge detail
3 - Glass lenses that illuminate the water feature by night
4 - Circular metal grill surrounding two trees

1 - *Brunnera macrophylla 'Jack Frost', Galium odoratum*
2 - *Brunnera macrophylla 'Jack Frost'*
3 - *Lamium maculatum, Galium odoratum, Brunnera macrophylla 'Jack Frost'*
4 - *Epimedium, Geranium macrorrhizum*
5 - *Luzula nivea, Brunnera macrophylla 'Jack Frost'*
6 - *Lamium maculatum, Bergenia*
7 - *Lamium maculatum, Geranium macrorrhizum*
8 - *Galium odoratum*
9 - Portland stone, steel edging, gravel mulch

Queen's Diamond Garden

Location:	Victoria
Site Area:	> 1,500 m^2
Completion:	2000
Designer:	Nigel Dunnet
Transport:	St. James's Park & Victoria Stations
Open:	24/7

Queen's Diamond Garden

Epimedium, Vinca minor, Luzula nivea, Brunnera macrophylla 'Jack Frost'

Queen's Diamond Garden

1

2

John Lewis Rain Garden

Location:	Westminster
Site Area:	< 500 m^2
Completion:	2015
Designer:	Nigel Dunnett
Transport:	St. James's Park Station
Open:	24/7

1 - *Alnus cordata* alongside planting that can tolerate wet weather, but also cope with potential dry conditions.
2 - Stainless steel storm water planter captures water runoff from the roof.

1

2

3

4

Pavilion Road

Location:	Chelsea
Site Area:	> 500 m^2
Completion:	2016
Designer:	Bradley-Hole Schoenaich Landscape
Transport:	Sloane Square Station
Open:	24/7

1 - *Diksonia antarctica, Cycas revoluta*

2 - *Trachycarpus fortunei* flowers

3 - *Cycas revolutam,* Yorkstone steps, steel handrail

4 - Stacked Italian lavastone and hardwood top stools

Pavilion Road

City of London

3

3. London – City of London

36
35
29
32
34
33
28
27
24
26
30
31
25

Carter Lane Gardens

Carter Lane Gardens

Location:	City of London
Site Area:	> 2,000 m^2
Completion:	2002
Designer:	Townshend Landscape Architects
Transport:	St. Paul's Station
Open:	24/7

1 - *Quercus palustris*
2 - Granite benches in-between layers of planting
3 - *Wisteria japonica*
4 - *Geranium phaeum*
5 - Bollard light
6 - Anti-skate stainless steel studs
7 - Granite benches in-between layers of planting and lawn
8 - Lawn and planted areas
9 - Steel tactile studs

Carter Lane Gardens

Carter Lane Gardens

1

2

3

4

Tower of London

Location:	City of London
Site Area:	> 1,000 m^2
Completion:	2004
Designer:	Stanton Williams
Transport:	Tower Hill Station
Open:	24/7

1 - Granite setts paving, granite benches
2 - Granite bench, *Plantanus x acerifolia*
3 - Granite steps
4 - Steps, clipped *Lonicera nitida*

Watling Street Gardens

Hakonechloa macra, Pachysandra terminalis, Convallaria majalis, Dryopteris filix-mas, multistem Betula utilis jacquemontii

1

2

3

4

Watling Street Gardens

Location:	City of London
Site Area:	> 1,500 m^2
Completion:	2000
Designer:	Elizabeth Banks Associates
Transport:	St. Paul's Station
Open:	24/7

1 - *Euphorbia characias subsp. wulfenii, Libertia grandiflora, Acer palmatum*
2 - *Hakonechloa macra*
3 - *Choisya ternata*
4 - *Rhaphiolepis umbellata*

Watling Street Gardens

Raised Yorkstone clad planter with bronze anti-skateboard studs *Euphorbia characias subsp. wulfenii, Libertia grandiflora, Acer palmatum*

St. Paul's Gardens

St. Paul's Gardens

Location:	City of London
Site Area:	> 500 m^2
Completion:	2008
Designer:	Purcell
Transport:	St. Paul's Station
Open:	6 am–8 pm/4 pm in winter

A combination of lawn and Purbeck stone paving and edging is used at St. Paul's South Churchyard to recreate the outline of the Chapter House.

Paternoster Square

Location:	City of London
Site Area:	> 2,000 m^2
Completion:	2003
Designer:	Whitfield Partners
Transport:	St. Paul's Station
Open:	24/7

Radial pattern of sandstone and light grey paving with a Corinthian column of Portland stone in the middle.

Finsbury Avenue Square

Location:	City of London
Site Area:	> 2,000 m^2
Completion:	2002
Designer:	Skidmore, Owings & Merrill
Transport:	Liverpool Street & Moorgate Stations
Open:	24/7

1 - Tree uplighter
2 - Stainless steel tree grill
3 - Anti-skate stainless steel studs
4 - Frosted LED lighting strips, slot drain
5 - Glass upstand
6 - Bespoke bench
7 - Glass upstand
8 - A grid of in-ground array of colour changing lamps
9 - Granite paving

Finsbury Avenue Square

Finsbury Avenue Square

Peter's Hill Steps

Peter's Hill Steps

Location:	City of London
Site Area:	> 1,000 m^2
Completion:	1997
Designer:	Charles Funke Associates
Transport:	St. Paul's & Blackfriars Stations
Open:	24/7

1 - *Gingko biloba*, Yorkstone paving

2 - Feathered flamed texture granite steps and ramp

Festival Gardens

1

2

3

4

Festival Gardens

Location:	City of London
Site Area:	> 1,500 m^2
Completion:	2012
Designer:	Worshipful Company of Gardeners
Transport:	St. Paul's Station
Open:	24/7

1 - Sunken lawn with wall fountain

2 - Pleached lime trees, *Sarcococca confusa, Lavandula augustifolia*

3 - Raised paved terrace with stone parapets and seating

4 - Pleached lime trees, *Sarcococca confusa, Lavandula augustifolia*

1

2

3

4

New Street Square

Location:	City of London
Site Area:	> 500 m^2
Completion:	2008
Designer:	Turkington Martin
Transport:	Chancery Lane & City Thameslink Stations
Open:	24/7

1 - Plinth water feature, benches and paving from Irish limestone, raised lawn and a group of oaks

2 - Green wall

3 - Stone clad steel frame benches, York-stone paving

4 - Cluster of *Gleditsia triacanthos*

Greyfriars Church Garden

The body of the church designed by Sir Christopher Wren at the end of the 17th century was destroyed during WW2.

1

2

3

4

Greyfriars Church Garden

Location:	City of London
Site Area:	> 500 m^2
Completion:	2011
Designer:	unknown
Transport:	St. Paul's Station
Open:	24/7

1 - Formal box hedge border and wooden pergolas provide garden structure
2 - Irises
3 - Wooden pergola with climbing plants
4 - Box hedge, *salvias* and *heuhera* perennial planting

Greyfriars Church Garden

Greyfriars Church Garden

1

2

3

4

One Coleman Street Gardens

Location:	City of London
Site Area:	< 500 m^2
Completion:	2007
Designer:	Townshend Landscape Architects
Transport:	Moorgate Station
Open:	24/7

1 - Granite stool, multistem *Amelanchier lamarckii,* box hedge

2 - Granite kerb, bollard lighting

3 - Lawn, multistem *Amelanchier lamarckii,*

4 - Timber bench surrounded with planting

Barbican Conservatory

Barbican Conservatory

Location:	Barbican
Site Area:	2,100 m^2
Completion:	1984
Designer:	Chamberlin, Powell and Bon
Transport:	Barbican Station
Open:	Sunday afternoons, some bank holidays

Barbican Conservatory

Barbican Conservatory

Barbican Roof Gardens

1

2

3

4

Barbican Roof Gardens

Location:	Barbican
Site Area:	> 5,000 m^2
Completion:	2013
Designer:	Nigel Dunnett
Transport:	Barbican Station
Open:	24/7

1 - *Lychnis coronaria 'Alba', Kniphopia 'Tawney King', Salvia nemerosa 'Caradonna', Verbena bonariensis, Euphorbia charavias, Sisyrinchium striatum, Alliums* seedheads

2 - *Lychnis chalcedonica, Phlomis russeliana*

3 - *Kniphopia 'Tawney King', Achillea 'Terracotta', Salvia nemerosa 'Caradonna'*

4 - *Melica ciliata, Lychnis coronaria 'Alba', Achillea 'Terracotta', Salvia nemerosa 'Caradonna', Sisyrinchium striatum*

Barbican Roof Gardens

East

4

4. London – East

44
49
46
43
47
38
45
52
53
48
50
36
41
40
51
39

Bishops Square

Fine picked mild grey granite paving, edge units, and polished seating edge

Bishops Square

Location:	Spitafields
Site Area:	> 6,000 m^2
Completion:	2010
Designer:	Townshend Landscape Architects
Transport:	Liverpool Street & Shoreditch High Street st.
Open:	24/7

1 - Laminated glass
2 - Square uplighter
3 - Stainless steel ashtray
4 - Granite setts, recessed manhole cover
5 - Circle uplighter, fine picked mild grey granite
6 - Lily pond, mild grey polished granite edge
7 - Lily pond
8 - Tacktile Yorkstone paving and step units
9 - Tree pit detail

Bishops Square

Lily pond, mild grey granite edge; Taxus baccata hedge and multistem *Amelanchier lamarckii*

Bow Riverside Path

Location:	Bow
Site Area:	< 5,000 m^2
Completion:	2011
Designer:	Adams & Sutherland Architects
Transport:	Bromley-by-Bow & Pudding Mill Lane Stations
Open:	24/7

A pedestrian walkway with Ekki hardwood spindles and Hi-Grip Plus non-slip deck

Baltimore Wharf

1 2 3 4 5 6 7 8 9

Baltimore Wharf

Location:	Isle of Dogs
Site Area:	< 5,000 m^2
Completion:	2010
Designer:	IN-EX Landscapes
Transport:	Crossharbour Station
Open:	24/7

1 - Polished granite water feature
2 - Recess lights in granite kerb
3 - Ground strip lighting
4 - Recess slot drain inspection chamber
5 - Polished black granite water feature
6 - Granite clad wall with light fitting
7 - *Prunus serrula, Sarcococca confusa, Pachysandra terminalis*
8 - Water feature detail
9 - Portable street furniture

Cartier Circle

Location:	Canary Wharf
Site Area:	> 500 m^2
Completion:	2011
Designer:	Townshend Landscape Architects
Transport:	Canary Wharf Station
Open:	24/7

Large bronze art-posts with top lights positioned across the clopped box maze inside a roundabout with a granite setts margin.

Jubilee Park

Jubilee Park

Serpentine raised water feature with *Metasequioa glytostroboides* at the bachground

1 - Dry stone wall
2 - *Cornus stolonifera 'Kelseys Dwarf'*
3 - *Pennisetum alopecuroides*
4 - Oak sleepers steps and resin-bound gravel
5 - Stainless steel street light
6 - Stainless steel bike rack
7 - Chiseled Belgium limestone texture
8 - Detail of dry stone wall
9 - Clipped *Fagus sylvatica* hedge

Jubilee Park

Location:	Canary Wharf
Site Area:	$< 10,000\ m^2$
Completion:	2002
Designer:	Wirtz International
Transport:	Canary Wharf Station
Open:	24/7

Jubilee Park

Granite paving, Belgium limestone clad retaining wall with split face top stone and groundcover *Cornus stolonifera 'Kelseys Dwarf'*

Jubilee Park

Jubilee Park

Tarmac path, Belgium limestone walls with *Pennisetum alopecuroides*, *Metasequioa glytostroboides* and multistem *Zelkova serrata*

Leonard Circus

Load-bearing StrataCell modular system ensures a greatly enhanced soil environment eliminating compaction and maintaining irrigation and ventilation.

Leonard Circus

Leonard Circus

Location:	Old Street
Site Area:	> 1,000 m^2
Completion:	2014
Designer:	Hackney Council
Transport:	Old Street Station
Open:	24/7

Shared space junction between Leonard and Paul Street. A patchwork of grey granite, Yorkstone and Italian porphyry paving in combination with urban trees planted using GreenBlue Urban load-bearing StrataCell modular system

Queen Elizabeth Olympic Park

Queen Elizabeth Olympic Park

Location:	Stratford
Site Area:	1,109 km^2
Completion:	2012
Designer:	LDA Design & Hargreaves Associate
Transport:	Stratford & Stratford International Stations
Open:	24/7

1–9 - Details of various timber seating areas throughout the park. Non-permeable resin bonded gravel surfaces are mixed with CEDEC footpath gravels by CED that form a firm but porous structure that retains moisture yet allows any excess to flow through.

Queen Elizabeth Olympic Park

Queen Elizabeth Olympic Park

Queen Elizabeth Olympic Park

Queen Elizabeth Olympic Park

Queen Elizabeth Olympic Park

Queen Elizabeth Olympic Park
Steep grassland bank with dominant *Eschscholzia californica* flowers

Queen Elizabeth Olympic Park

Irrigation/aeration and guying products by GreenBlue Urban maintain the longevity and stability of the carefully chosen trees.

Queen Elizabeth Olympic Park

Athletes Village

Athletes Village

Location:	Olympic Park London
Site Area:	151,000 m^2
Completion:	2012
Designer:	Vogt Landschaftsarchitekten
Transport:	Stratford International Station
Open:	24/7

Athletes Village

Athletes Village

Athletes Village

Raised planters with biodiversity rich lawn

Athletes Village

Athletes Village

Three Mills Green

Location:	Lea Valley
Site Area:	> 20,000 m^2
Completion:	2011
Designer:	Churchman Landscape Architects
Transport:	Bromley-By-Bow Station
Open:	24/7

1

2

3

4

Ulysses Place

1 - Resin-bonded gravel, combined tree pits and curved retaining wall

2 - Wall and seats from reconstituted pigmented stone

3 - Bespoke letters

4 - Groups of uplighters along the curved wall

Location:	Stratford
Site Area:	< 2,500 m^2
Completion:	2012
Designer:	Vogt Landschaftsarchitekten
Transport:	Stratford International Station
Open:	24/7

Ulysses Place

Ulysses Place

Ulysses Place

1 - In-situ concrete, exposed aggregate concrete kerb, tarmac surface
2 - Precast concrete seats
3 - Precast concrete cycle lane sign
4 - Reclaimed granite setts
5 - Reused brick rubble
6 - Reclaimed brick and in-situ concrete bench detail
7 - Weathered steel signage
8 - Tarmac with rolled in gravel
9 - Precast concrete markers

Greenway

Location:	Hackney
Site Area:	7 km
Completion:	2011
Designer:	Adams & Sutherland Architects
Transport:	Pudding Mill Lane Station
Open:	24/7

1

2

3

4

5

1 - Stainless steel benches clad with hardwood

2 - *Lonicera nitida*, steel balustrade with cables and hardwood handrail

3 - Granite and hardwood decking public promenade

4 - Granite bench with hardwood timber seating surface

5 - Raised oval lawn, bespoke concrete benches, *Hedera helix* and *Betula pendula* planting

New Providence Wharf

Location:	Poplar
Site Area:	< 3,000 m^2
Completion:	2007
Designer:	IN-EX Landscapes
Transport:	Blackwall Station
Open:	24/7

New Providence Wharf

Sloping terraced lawn area

1

2

3

4

5

6

7

8

9

Drapers Field

1 - Granite gabions, wildflower turf, brick wall
2 - Steel bench
3 - Stained concrete retaining wall
4 - Bicycle shelter
5 - Raised kerb, wildflower turf
6 - Stainless steel bollard
7 - *Pinus sylvestris* grid planting
8 - Weathering steel
9 - Multistem street tree planting

Location:	Waltham Forest
Site Area:	< 35,000 m^2
Completion:	2014
Designer:	Kinnear Landscape Architects
Transport:	Leyton Station
Open:	24/7

Drapers Field

The Crystal

1

2

3

4

The Crystal

Location:	Royal Docks
Site Area:	< 18,000 m^2
Completion:	2012
Designer:	Townshend Landscape Architects
Transport:	Royal Victoria Station
Open:	24/7

1 - Raised brick planters, timber seating, resin-bound gravel
2 - *Verbena bonariensis*
3 - Green oak planted with galvanised steel corners
4 - Brick paving

Wood Wharf

Location:	Isle of Dogs
Site Area:	< 10,000 m^2
Completion:	2012
Designer:	Townshend Landscape Architects
Transport:	Canary Wharf Station
Open:	24/7

St Andrew's Housing

1

2

3

4

St Andrew's Housing

Location:	Bromley-by-Bow
Site Area:	5,300 m^2
Completion:	2013
Designer:	Townshend Landscape Architects
Transport:	Bromley-by-Bow Station
Open:	24/7

1 - Raised brick planters, timber seating, resin-bound gravel

2 - *Thymus vulgaris*

3 - *Origanum majorana, Lavandula angustifolia*

4 - Clipped box hedge

Crossrail Station Rooftop Garden

1

2

3

4

Crossrail Station Rooftop Garden

Location:	Canary Wharf
Site Area:	5,300 m^2
Completion:	2015
Designer:	Gillespies LLP
Transport:	West India Quay & Poplar Stations
Open:	Daily during station operating hours

1 - Granite and resin-bonded gravel paths separating slow and fast human flows

2 - *Pachysandra terminalis, Hosta,* fern

3 - *Pachysandra terminalis,* fern

4 - Ferns

Crossrail Station Rooftop Garden

Crossrail Station Rooftop Garden

Modular structural StrataCells were integrated into the scheme providing optimum load bearing and root welfare environments

West

5

5. London – West

59
64
58
63
60
54
55
57
61
56
→
62

Princess Diana Memorial Fountain

Princess Diana Memorial Fountain

Location:	Hyde Park
Site Area:	> 3,000 m^2
Completion:	2004
Designer:	Gustafson Porter + Bowman
Transport:	Knightsbridge & Lancaster Gate Stations
Open:	10 am–4/8 pm

1–9 - Cornish granite was cut using digital technology. Detailed grooves and channels combine with air jets to animate the water.

Princess Diana Memorial Fountain

Exhibition Road

28 bespoke tapering twenty-metre steel lighting masts which define the centre of the carriageway

Exhibition Road

Location:	South Kensington
Site Area:	22,000 m^2
Completion:	2012
Designer:	Dixon Jones Architects
Transport:	South Kensington Station
Open:	24/7

1 - Granite setts, granite kerb and tactile warning steel studs
2 - Steel bollards
3 - Steel tactile studs, steel edge
4 - Tactile granite paving setts, drainage channel
5 - Stainless steel demarcation studs
6 - Granite setts in diamond shape pattern
7 - Tactile Scoutmoor Yorkstone paving
8 - Light column base
9 - Bike racks

1

2

3

4

5

6

7

8

9

1 - Cafe temporary seating
2 - Granite kerb informal seating edge
3 - Timber benches and bike racks
4 - On-street parking
5 - Diamond-shaped paving pattern
6 - Timber benches
7 - Tactile paving demarcating strictly pedestrian areas
8 - Continuous drainage channel
9 - Granite setts paving for vehicle and pedestrian use

Exhibition Road

Shared surface street

Hammersmith Grove

Stachys byzantina, Liriope muscari, Gaura lindheimeri, Panicum virgatum, Lavandula angustifolia 'Hidcote', box and yew hedge

Hammersmith Grove

Location:	Hammersmith
Site Area:	< 1,000 m^2
Completion:	2012
Designer:	Planit – IE
Transport:	Hammersmith Station
Open:	24/7

1 - Limestone bollards, multistem *Carpinus betulus*
2 - *Eryngium yuccifolium*, box hedge
3 - Steel tactile studs, steel edge
4 - *Liriope muscari,* tree uplighter
5 - Stainless steel demarcation studs
6 - Granite paving, flamed and bush hammered finish
7 - Gravel mulch
8 - *Stachys byzantina, Liriope muscari, Lavandula angustifolia 'Hidcote'*
9 - Granite paving

Hammersmith Grove

multistem *Carpinus betulus*, *Liriope muscari*

Hammersmith Grove

Stachys byzantina, Liriope muscari, Gaura lindheimeri, Panicum virgatum, Lavandula angustifolia 'Hidcote', yew hedge, limestone planter

1

2

3

4

John Madejski Garden

Location:	South Kensington
Site Area:	< 1,000 m^2
Completion:	2005
Designer:	Kim Wilkie
Transport:	South Kensington Station
Open:	10 am–5.45 pm daily, except Christmas

1 - Oval pool with feathered steps
2 - Yorkstone paving edge
3 - Glass planter
4 - *Geranium maderense*

John Madejski Garden

Liquidambar styraciflua with underplanted irises

1

2

3

4

Paddington

Location:	Paddington
Site Area:	> 1,000 m^2
Completion:	2005
Designer:	Townshend Landscape Architects
Transport:	Paddington & Edware Road Stations
Open:	24/7

1–4 Amphitheatre with lawn terraces

1

2

3

4

Merchant Square

Location:	Paddington
Site Area:	< 1,000 m^2
Completion:	2016
Designer:	Townshend Landscape Architects
Transport:	Paddington & Edware Road Stations
Open:	24/7

1 - Jets water feature
2 - Bespoke seating detail
3 - Steel and granite edge, box hedge
4 - Bespoke timber bench

1

2

3

4

Kensington Palace Garden

Location:	Kensington Garden
Site Area:	> 3,000 m^2
Completion:	2012
Designer:	Todd Longstaffe-Gowan
Transport:	Queensway & High Street Kensington Stations
Open:	24/7

1 - Meandering walk through hornbeam hedge
2 - Steel edge and resin-bound gravel steps
3 - Galvanised steel edge detail
4 - Clipped *Carpinus betulus* hedge

Kensington Palace Garden

Lime tree tunnel with resin-bound gravel path edged with galvanized steel

1

2

3

4

5

6

7

8

9

1 - Limestone paving
2 - Pleached lime trees
3 - Limestone paving and water feature drain detail
4 - One of the 15 water jets with integrated warm white halogen lights
5 - Quote engraved in stone
6 - Water feature stainless steel grating detail
7 - Temporary cafe seating
8 - Permanent stone seats
9 - Limestone paving

Lyric Square

Location:	Hammersmith
Site Area:	> 1,000 m^2
Completion:	2005
Designer:	GROSS.MAX.
Transport:	Hammersmith Station
Open:	24/7

Lyric Square

Rootstein Hopkins Parade Ground

Mast street lamps, *Liquidambar styraciflua*

Rootstein Hopkins Parade Ground

Location:	Chelsea
Site Area:	3,500 m^2
Completion:	2011
Designer:	Planet Earth
Transport:	Pimlico Station
Open:	24/7

A unique LED-lit geometric grid defines the space, which for evening events, can be programmed to complement and enhance the activities, illuminating the Parade Ground in sections and sequences to create stunning effects.

Marylebone Road Green Wall

Euphorbia 'Humpty Dumpty', Heuchera 'Plum Pudding', Acorus 'Ogon', Geranium 'Max Frei', Erysimum 'Bowles Mauve', Veronica 'Waterperry Blue', Vinca minor 'La Grave', Waldsteinia ternate

Marylebone Road Green Wall

Location:	Edgware
Site Area:	200 m^2
Completion:	2011
Designer:	Biotecture
Transport:	Edgware Road Station
Open:	24/7

Heuchera 'Plum Pudding', Acorus 'Ogon', Lavandula 'Munsted', Carex testacea, Euphorbia 'Humpty Dumpty', Veronica 'Waterperry Blue', Vinca minor 'La Grave', Waldsteinia ternate, Euonymus 'Emerald n' Gold', Euonymus 'Emerald Gaiety'

Kingdom Street

1

2

3

4

Kingdom Street

Location:	Paddington
Site Area:	> 5,000 m^2
Completion:	2017
Designer:	Townshend Landscape Architects
Transport:	Warwick Avenue & Paddington Stations
Open:	24/7

1 - Meandering Yorkstone path between mounded landscape

2 - Chunky solid hardwood bench

3 - Tooth-shaped Yorkstone paving edge, *Geranium phaeum*

4 - Corten light bollard

South-West

6

6. London – South-West

71
69
68
65
70
66
67

1

2

3

4

The Kerb Garden

Location:	Stockwell
Site Area:	$< 500\ m^2$
Completion:	2013
Designer:	The Edible Bus Stop
Transport:	Stockwell Station
Open:	24/7

1 - Pleached fig tree, perforated metal fence

2 - *Kniphofia rooperi*

3 - Reclaimed granite kerbs created raised beds

The Kerb Garden

1 - Granite steps

2 - *Verbena bonariensis, Anemanthele lessoniana, Lythrum salicaria*

3 - *Lavandula, Crocosmia*

4 - *Verbena bonariensis*

5 - Stepping stone water feature

6 - Granite seat, *Fagus* sylvatica hedge

7 - Granite water feature

8 - *Fuchsia riccartonii, Osmanthus burkwoodii, Hydrangea*

9 - Granite water feature

Emerald Square

Location:	Roehampton
Site Area:	< 2,000 m^2
Completion:	2010
Designer:	Schoenaich Landscape Architects
Transport:	Barnes Station
Open:	24/7

Emerald Square

1

2

3

4

Gillis Square

Location:	Roehampton
Site Area:	< 1,000 m^2
Completion:	2013
Designer:	Schoenaich Landscape Architects
Transport:	Barnes Station
Open:	24/7

1 - *Rosa 'Kent', Viburnum davidii,* pleached lime trees, grey granite and water feature
2 - Raised granite kerb
3 - *Rosa 'Kent', Viburnum davidii*
4 - Hardwood timber benches

Gillis Square

Sackler Bridge

Sackler Bridge

Location:	KEW Gardens
Site Area:	< 100 m^2
Completion:	2006
Designer:	John Pawson
Transport:	Kew Gardens Station
Open:	10 am–10.45 pm daily

The walkway is formed of rhythmic bands of black granite with cast bronze uprights that form the balustrade.

Treetop Walkway at KEW

Treetop Walkway at KEW

Location:	KEW Gardens
Site Area:	$< 500\ m^2$
Completion:	2008
Designer:	Marks Barfield Architects
Transport:	Kew Gardens Station
Open:	10 am–10.45 pm daily

1 - The walkway is a 200-metre-long string of twelve modular walkway trusses at eighteen metres high

2 - 1.3-metre-high handrails are laminated with sweet chestnut wood

3 - Single stage hydraulic lift with a glazed panoramic lift car with 118 steps

4 - Weathering Steel structure and mesh

Treetop Walkway at KEW

Treetop Walkway at KEW

Windrush Square

Location:	Brixton
Site Area:	> 5,000 m^2
Completion:	2008
Designer:	GROSS.MAX.
Transport:	Brixton Station
Open:	24/7

Existing London plane, a mix of limestone slabs and Neland Johannesberg pavers, Boston seats cluster by Santa & Cole

Trafalgar Place

1

2

3

4

Trafalgar Place

Location:	Elephant & Castle
Site Area:	> 3,000 m^2
Completion:	2017
Designer:	Randle Siddeley
Transport:	Elephant & Castle Station
Open:	24/7

1 - Box hedges with betula

2 - Swale

3 - Ferns, *Hosta, Pachysandra terminalis, Heuhera*

4 - Box balls, *Ginkgo biloba*

South-East

7

7. London – South-East

85
84
78
82
80
81
76
77
74
79
86
72
83
75
87
89
73
88

Cutter Lane

1

2

3

4

5

6

Cutter Lane

Location:	Greenwich Peninsula
Site Area:	> 1,000 m²
Completion:	2012
Designer:	Aedas
Transport:	North Greenwich Station
Open:	24/7

1 - Tactile concrete paving, cropped granite setts, slot drain
2 - Shared surface street
3 - Tactile concrete paving, cropped granite setts, slot drain
4 - Concrete paving
5 - Concrete paving
6 - Concrete paving

Cutty Sark Gardens

Cutty Sark Gardens

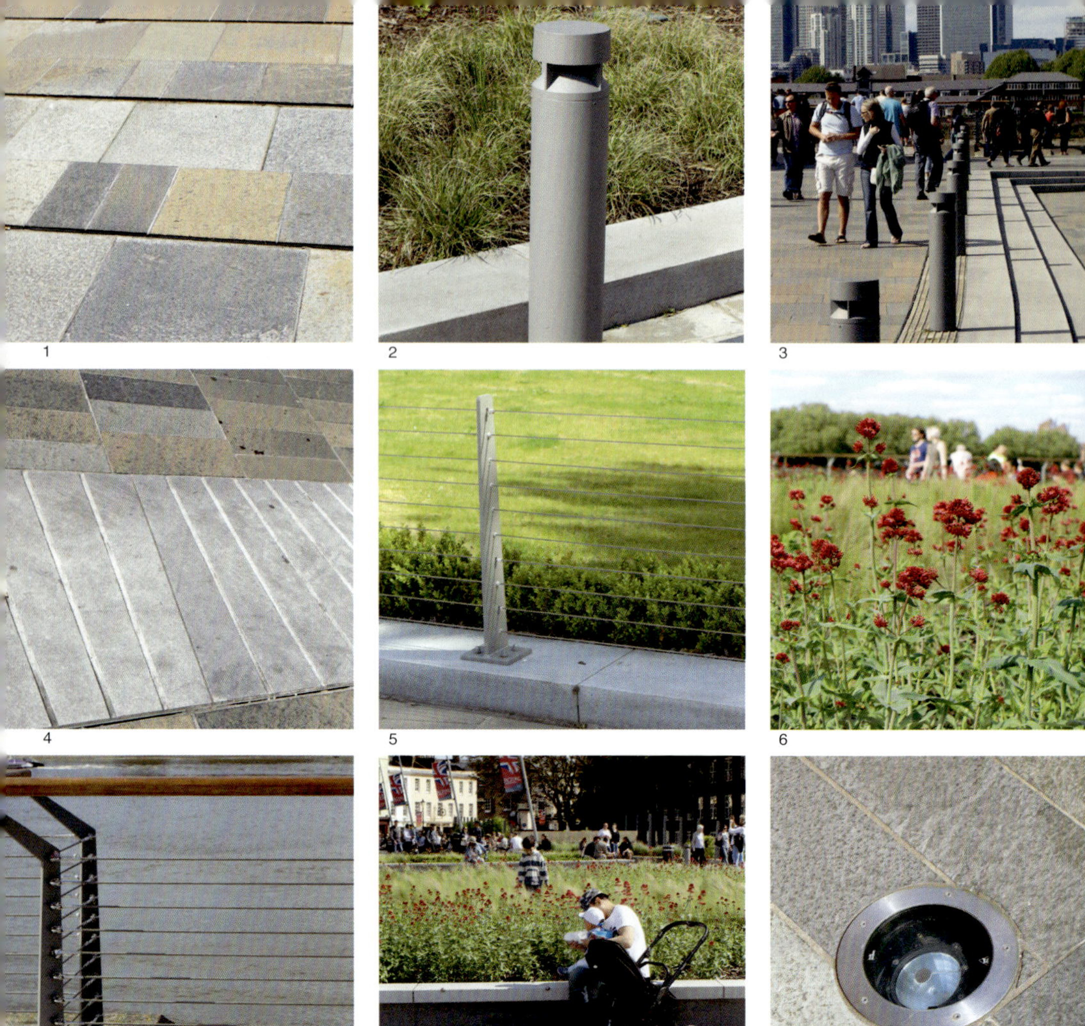

1 - Slate recessed water feature
2 - Light bollard
3 - Light bollards and steps
4 - Slate and granite paving
5 - Wire rope balustrade
6 - *Centranthus ruber*
7 - Wire rope balustrade with hardwood handrail
8 - Raised planter
9 - Ground uplighter

Cutty Sark Gardens

Location:	Greenwich
Site Area:	19,000 m^2
Completion:	2009
Designer:	OKRA
Transport:	Cutty Sark for Maritime Greenwich Station
Open:	24/7

Cutty Sark Gardens

Gibbon's Rent

1

2

3

4

Gibbon's Rent

Location:	Southwark
Site Area:	< 500 m^2
Completion:	2012
Designer:	Andrew Burns, Sarah Eberle
Transport:	London Bridge Station
Open:	24/7

1 - Concrete pipes used as planters
2 - Local community planting
3 - Tarmac path, scattered furniture and planters
4 - *Rosmarinus officinalis 'Prostratus'*

Gibbon's Rent

Greenwich Peninsula Ecology Park

Greenwich Peninsula Ecology Park

Greenwich Peninsula Ecology Park

1

2

3

4

5

6

7

8

9

Greenwich Peninsula Ecology Park

Location:	Greenwich Peninsula
Site Area:	110,000 m^2
Completion:	2002
Designer:	Atkins, Desvigne & Dalnoky
Transport:	North Greenwich Station
Open:	10 am–5 pm, Wed–Sun

1 - Granite steps with resin-bonded intervals
2 - Low fence made of branches
3 - PAR oak balustrade
4 - Native trees and shrub planting
5 - Native trees and shrub planting
6 - Granite setts
7 - Oak bridge and balustrade
8 - Man-made fresh water pond
9 - Garden pavilion with low maintenance green roof

Jubilee Garden

Jubilee Garden

Jubilee Garden

Jubilee Garden

Location:	Southbank
Site Area:	120,000 m^2
Completion:	2012
Designer:	WEST 8
Transport:	Waterloo and Embankment Stations
Open:	24/7

1 - Silver Grey granite seating unit by CED with stainless stell bollards
2 - Alliums
3 - *Heuchera*
4 - Silver grey granite edge unit
5 - Hardwood bench
6 - Flamed and cropped Silver Grey granite setts by CED
7 - *Heuchera*
8 - Lampost
9 - Silver Grey granite corner seating unit by CED

Jubilee Garden

Majority of soft surface areas covered with durable Arena Sport Turf with over 50 new trees, including: *Taxodium distichum, Quercus palustris, Tilia platyphyllos, Quercus robur and Luquidambar*

Jubilee Garden

Combination of granite setts both flamed and cropped and granite seating/edging units

Jubilee Garden

More London

Location:	Southwark
Site Area:	> 200,000 m^2
Completion:	2010
Designer:	Townshend Landscape Architects
Transport:	London Bridge and Tower Hill Stations
Open:	24/7

More London

1 - Jets water feature

2 - Multistem *betula* and clipped *buxus* hedge

3 - Water reel

4 - Flame-textured Carlow Blue limestone water feature edge

5 - Inner courtyard with stainless steel furniture

6 - *Amelanchier lamarckii,* clipped *buxus* hedge

7 - Stainless steel bollard

8 - Carlow Blue limestone stone seats

9 - Flame-textured Carlow Blue limestone paving

NEO Bankside

NEO Bankside

Location:	Southwark
Site Area:	> 5,000 m^2
Completion:	2012
Designer:	Gillespies, Growth Industry
Transport:	Blackfriars and Southwark Stations
Open:	24/7

1 - Staggered betula planting with *Euphorbia robbiae, Anemanthele lessoniana, Luzula, Hypericum*
2 - *Asplenium scolopendrium*
3 - *Soleirolia soleirolii and path edge detail*
4 - Stepping stones
5 - Granite steps
6 - *Helenium 'Moorheim beauty', Molinia Caerulea 'Moorhexe'*
7 - Lawn edge, hoggin, galvanized steel edge
8 - Tree uplighter within resin-bound gravel
9 - Pebbles and granite stone detail

NEO Bankside

NEO Bankside

NEO Bankside

NEO Bankside

Potters Fields Park

1 2 3 4 5 6 7 8 9

Potters Fields Park

Location:	Southwark
Site Area:	< 5,000 m^2
Completion:	2007
Designer:	GROSS.MAX.
Transport:	London bridge and Tower Hill Stations
Open:	24/7

1 - *Knautia Macedonica*
2 - *Echinacea 'Tennesseensis', Salvia × sylvestris 'Rhapsody in Blue', Sesleria autumnalis*
3 - *Echinacea 'Tennesseensis'*
4 - *Geranium 'Claridge Druce', Sesleria autumnalis*
5 - *Helenium 'Moorheim beauty'*
6 - *Helenium 'Moorheim beauty', Molinia Caerulea 'Moorhexe'*
7 - *Sesleria autumnalis*
8 - *Brunnera Macrophylla*
9 - *Buxus* clipped hedge, *Baptisia Leucantha*

Potters Fields Park

1 - Boston seats cluster by Santa & Cole
2 - Granite concrete kerb
3 - Granite bench etched with floral pattern
4 - *Geranium 'Claridge Druce', Sesleria autumnalis*
5 - LED light post
6 - Strip light fitting within clay brick paving
7 - Steel gate entrance detail
8 - Moon bench detail by Santa & Cole
9 - Garden gate detail with floral pattern

Potters Fields Park

Queen Mary Walk

Queen Mary Walk

1

2

3

4

Queen Mary Walk

Location:	Southwark
Site Area:	< 2,000 m^2
Completion:	2008
Designer:	GROSS.MAX.
Transport:	Waterloo and Embankment Stations
Open:	24/7

1 - Limestone stepped access to the shops and restaurants

2 - Bespoke feature light post

3 - Dark limestone steps with grey granite margins

4 - Limestone drainage channel cover

Queen Mary Walk

Queen Elizabeth Hall Roof Garden

Queen Elizabeth Hall Roof Garden

Location:	Southbank
Site Area:	> 500 m^2
Completion:	2011
Designer:	Jane Knight, Paul Stone
Transport:	Waterloo & Embankment Stations
Open:	10 am–10 pm

Tate Modern

1

2

3

4

Tate Modern

1 - Areas of lawn and closely planted *Betula pendula*

2 - Curved retaining wall

3 - Concrete benches wrapped in rubber sheets

4 - Pigmented concrete wall with exposed flint aggregate

Location:	Southbank
Site Area:	> 10,000 m^2
Completion:	2010
Designer:	VOGT
Transport:	Southbank Station
Open:	24/7

Tate Modern

Tate Modern

Thames Barrier Park

1 - *Anemone × hybrida*
2 - *Anemone × hybrida 'Honorine Jobert'*
3 - *Rudbeckia fulgida*
4 - *Acanthus mollis*
5 - *Echinacea purpurea*
6 - *Achillea filipendulina*
7 - *Agapanthus*
8 - *Calamagrostis x acutiflora 'Karl Foerster'*
9 - *Achillea filipendulina*

Thames Barrier Park

Location:	Silvertown
Site Area:	> 70,000 m^2
Completion:	2000
Designer:	Patel Taylor, Groupe Signes, Alan Provost
Transport:	Pontoon Dock Station
Open:	7 am–7.15 pm

Thames Barrier Park

Thames Barrier Park

Thames Barrier Park

1 - Concrete wall covered in *Vitis*
2 - Bridge, balustrade and handrail intersection
3 - Stainless steel wire balustrade
4 - Clipped *Lonicera nitida*, stainless steel wire balustrade
5 - Galvanised steel fence
6 - Hardwood timber bench with galvanised steel handrests
7 - Concrete steps with a handrail
8 - Concrete wall covered in *Vitis*
9 - Wall of clipped *Lonicera nitida*

National Theatre

1

2

3

4

National Theatre

Location:	Southbank
Site Area:	< 1,000 m^2
Completion:	2015
Designer:	GROSS.MAX.
Transport:	Waterloo, Embankment Stations
Open:	24/7

1 - Tio chairs and table by Massproductions, galvanized metal wire covered with a polyester powder coat, galvanized light stands, hardwood decking

2 - *Stipa gigantea*

3 - Stained timber bench edge

4 - Hardwood timber bench corner detail

National Theatre

The Magis Air Armchair by Jasper Morrison, raised planter with black stained timber seating edge, *Stipa gigantea* and *alliums*

National Theatre

Luzula nivea, Pittosporum tobira, alliums, Hakonechloa macra and multistem birches

National Theatre

Luzula nivea, Pittosporum tobira, alliums, Hakonechloa macra and multistem birches in concrete planters

The Edmond J. Safra Fountain Court

Location:	Temple
Site Area:	$< 5,000$ m^2
Completion:	2000
Designer:	Dixon Jones
Transport:	Temple Station
Open:	24/7

A grid of 55 jets of water springs up to six meters high directly from the surface of the tumbled granite setts.

Greenwood Theatre Pocket Park

Erigeron karvinskianus, Foeniculum vulgare 'Purpureum', Erysimum 'Bowles's Mauve', Holboellia latifolia, Akebia quinata

1

2

3

4

Greenwood Theatre Pocket Park

Location:	Southwark
Site Area:	< 500 m^2
Completion:	2015
Designer:	Joe Swift, Dame Zandra Rhodes, Cityscapes
Transport:	London Bridge Station
Open:	24/7

1 - In-situ concrete planters with integrated seating

2 - Painted I-beams and brick walls

3 - A combination of perennial planting and climbers supported by stainless steel cables

4 - Hardwood timber seat, galvanized steel support, in-situ concrete edge

Burgess Park

CEDEC gravel by CED provides porous surface around the exisitng treees without affecting the pH value of the surrounding soil.

Burgess Park

Location:	Southwark
Site Area:	560,000 m^2
Completion:	2012
Designer:	LDA Design
Transport:	Elephant & Castle Station
Open:	24/7

1 - Tarmac path
2 - Informal timber play elements
3 - Species-rich lawn
4 - *Anemone pulsatilla*
5 - *Euphorbia palustris*
6 - *Brunnera macrophylla*
7 - *Alliaria petiolata*
8 - *Lunaria annua*
9 - *Camassia leichtlinii*

Kidbrooke Village Masterplan

1

2

3

4

Kidbrooke Village Masterplan

Location:	Kidbrooke
Site Area:	350,000 m^2
Completion:	ongoing
Designer:	Lifschutz Davidson Sandilands
Transport:	Kidbrooke Station
Open:	24/7

1 - Bespoke signage
2 - Raised corten planter, timber bench
3 - Brick paving
4 - Light fittings on a post
5 - Balustrade with stainless steel wire mesh
6 - Corten bollard
7 - Granite paving
8 - Underground services box for the market stalls
9 - Corten gully

Deptford Market Yard

Location:	Deptford
Site Area:	> 5,000 m^2
Completion:	2017
Designer:	Farrer Huxley Associates
Transport:	Deptford Station
Open:	24/7

Deptford Market Yard

Deptford Market Yard

Deptford Market Yard

References

ATKINS
Euston Tower
286 Euston Road
London
NW1 3AT
www.atkinsglobal.com

Adams & Sutherland Architects
Studio 1K
Highgate Business Centre
33 Greenwood Place
London
NW5 1LB
www.adams-sutherland.co.uk

AECOM
Aldgate Tower
2 Leman Street
London
E1 8FA
http://www.aecom.com/

Architects Network
15 Countess Road
London
NW5 2NS
www.architectsnetwork.co.uk

BDP
16 Brewhouse Yard
Clerkenwell
London
EC1V 4LJ
www.bdp.com

Biotecture
The Old Dairy, Ham Farm
Main Road
Bosham
PO18 8EH
www.biotecture.uk.com

Blair Associates Architecture
88 Golden Lane
London
EC1Y 0UA
blairaarch.com

Bradley-Hole Schoenaich
Landscape
Greystone House
Sudbrook Lane
Richmond
TW10 7AT
bhsla.co.uk

Charles Funke Associates
79–81 High Street
Godalming
GU7 1AW
charlesfunke.com

Churchman Landscape Architects
3.04 Chester House
Kennington Park
1–3 Brixton Road
London
SW9 6DE
www.churchmanlandscapearchitects.co.uk

Cityscapes
SHED Studio 2
8 Lee Street
London
E8 4DY
cityscapes.org.uk

Clarke Associates
1–5 Offord St
London
N1 1DH
www.clarkeassociates.cc

Dan Pearson Studio
The Nursery, The Chandlery
50 Westminster Bridge Road
London
SE1 7QY
www.danpearsonstudio.com

Debbie Schiesser I Arlington Enterprises
1–3 Charlotte St
London
W1T 1RD
www.arlingtonenterprises.co.uk

Dixon Jones Limited
2–3 Hanover Yard
Noel Road
London
N1 8YA
+44 (0)20 7483 8888
www.dixonjones.co.uk

East
4th floor
149–59 Old Street
London
EC1V 9HX
www.east.uk.com

EDCO Design
15 Knights Park
Kingston Upon Thames,
Surrey,
KT1 2QH
www.edcodesign.net

Farrer Huxley Associates
Unit 11, Union Wharf
23 Wenlock Road
London
N1 7SB
www.fha.co.uk

Gillespies
1 St John's Square
London
EC1M 4DH
www.gillespies.co.uk

GROSS.MAX.
6 Waterloo Place
Edinburgh
EH1 3EG
www.grossmax.com

Gustafson Porter + Bowman
1 Cobham Mews
London
NW1 9SB
www.gp-b.com

Hargreaves Associates
970 Tennessee Street
San Francisco
CA 94107
www.hargreaves.com

HOK
Qube
90 Whitfield Street
London
W1T 4EZ
www.hok.com

In-Ex Landscapes
6 Scott House
Admirals Way
Canary Wharf
London
E14 9UG
in-exlandscapes.com

J & L Gibbons
19 Swan Yard
London
N1 1SD
jlg-london.com

John Pawson
Unit B, York Central
70–78 York Way
London
N1 9AG
www.johnpawson.com

Kim Wilkie
16 Bank Chambers
25 Jermyn Street
London
SW1Y 6HR
www.kimwilkie.com

Kinnear Landscape Architects
3rd Floor West
1–3 Coate Street
London
E2 9AG
kland.co.uk

LDA Design
New Fetter place
8–10 New Fetter Lane
London
EC4A 1AZ
www.lda-design.co.uk

Marks Barfield Architects
50 Bromell's Road
London
SW4 0BG
www.marksbarfield.com

Neial Ayling
www.neilayling.com

Nigel Dunnett
www.nigeldunnett.com

OKRA LANDSCHAPSARCHI-
TECTEN
Oudegracht 23
3511 AB
Utrecht
Netherlands
www.okra.nl

Patel Taylor
48 Rawstorne Street
London
EC1V 7ND
www.pateltaylor.co.uk

Piet Oudolf
Broekstraat 17
6999 DE
Hummelo
Netherlands
oudolf.com

Planet Earth LTD
planetearthltd.co

Planit IE
Waterside
44–48 Wharf Road
London
N1 7UX
www.planit-ie.com

PLP Architecture
Bex House 4
2–47 Minories
London
EC3N 1DY
www.plparchitecture.com

PURCELL
15 Bermondsey Square
Tower Bride Road
London
SE1 3UN
purcelluk.com

Randall Sidley
3 Palmerston Court
Palmerston Way
London
SW8 4AJ
randlesiddeley.co.uk

remapp Landscape Architects
remapp.co.uk

SOM
The Broadgate Tower
20 Primrose Street
London
EC2A 2EW
www.som.com

Stanton Williams
36 Graham Street
London
N1 8GJ
www.stantonwilliams.com

Todd Longstaffe-Gowan Landscape Design
3rd floor Greenhill House
Greenhill Rents
90–93 Cowcross Street
London
EC1M 6BF
www.tlg-landscape.co.uk

Townshend Landscape Architects
1E Zetland House
5–25 Scrutton Street
London
EC2A 4HJ
www.townshendla.com

Turkington Martin
3.05 Chester House
Kennington Park Business Centre
1–3 Brixton Road
London
SW9 6DE
www.turkingtonmartin.com

Vogt Landscape Limited
Unit 9, New North House
Canonbury Yard
190 New North Road
London
N1 7BJ
www.vogt-la.com

West 8 urban design & landscape architecture
Schiehaven 13M
3024 EC Rotterdam
The Netherlands
www.west8.nl

Wirtz International
Botermelkdijk 464
2900 Schoten
België
www.wirtznv.be

Index

Acknowledgments

Main Supporters:

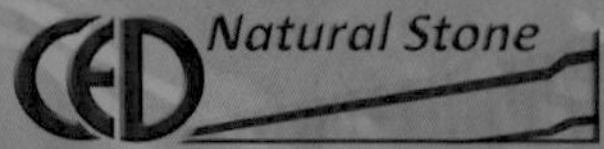

CED LTD
728 London Road
West Thurrock
Grays
Essex
RM20 3LU

01708 867237
www.ced.ltd.uk

GreenBlue Urban
Northpoint
Compass Park
Junction Road
Bodiam TN32 5BS

0800 018 7797
www.greenblue.com

Special thank you to:

Agnieszka Bak, Anja Bippus, Brita von Schoenaich, Guillaume Baltz, Michael Heap, Paul Bourel

Imprint

Cover: Vladimir Guculak

Design and setting: Vladimir Guculak
Lithography: Vladimir Guculak
Printing and binding: Belvédère, Oosterbeek, the Netherlands

Bibliographic information published by the Deutsche Nationalbibliothek
The Deutsche Nationalbibliothek lists this publication in the Deutsche Nationalbibliografie; detailed bibliographic data are available on the Internet at http://dnb.d-nb.de

jovis Verlag GmbH
Kurfürstenstrasse 15/16
10785 Berlin

www.jovis.de

jovis books are available worldwide in select bookstores. Please contact your nearest bookseller or visit www.jovis.de for information concerning your local distribution.

ISBN 978-3-86859-396-9